05/2011

Tim Horton

From Stanley Cups to Coffee Cups

This little book about a larger-than-life athlete and entrepreneur
is dedicated to all the students and teachers
who work hard every day to rise above challenges
in their search for success and personal fulfillment.

Don Quinlan

Published in Canada by Fitzhenry & Whiteside, 195 Allstate Parkway, Markham, Ontario L3R 4T8

Published in the United States by Fitzhenry & Whiteside, 311 Washington Street
Brighton, Massachusetts 02135

www.fitzhenry.ca   godwit@fitzhenry.ca

10 9 8 7 6 5 4 3 2 1

Library and Archives Canada Cataloguing in Publication
Quinlan, Don, 1947-
Tim Horton: from Stanley Cups to coffee cups / Don Quinlan.
Includes bibliographical references and index.
ISBN 978-1-55455-148-4 (bound).–ISBN 978-1-55455-046-3 (pbk.)
1. Horton, Tim, 1930-1974–Juvenile literature.   2. Hockey
players–Canada–Biography–Juvenile literature.   I. Title.
GV848.5.H58Q55 2009   j796.962092   C2009-904892-2

Publisher Cataloging-in-Publication Data (U.S.)
Quinlan, Don.
Tim Horton: from Stanley cups to coffee cups / Don Quinlan.
[72] p.: ill., photos (chiefly col.), maps; cm.
Includes bibliographical references and index.

Summary: Horton's life from his childhood in the hard-scrabble Ontario north, to the
National Hockey League, four Stanley Cups with the Maple Leafs, and his ventures as a
successful businessman.
ISBN: 978-1-55455-148-4
ISBN: 978-1-55455-046-3 (pbk.)

1. Hockey players – Canada – Biography – Juvenile literature.   I. Title.
796.962/092 dc22   GV848.5.H67Q56   2009

Fitzhenry & Whiteside acknowledges with thanks the Canada Council for the Arts, and the
Ontario Arts Council for their support of our publishing program. We acknowledge the financial
support of the Government of Canada through the Book Publishing Industry Development
Program (BPIDP) for our publishing activities.

 Canada Council   Conseil des Arts
for the Arts   du Canada

 ONTARIO ARTS COUNCIL
CONSEIL DES ARTS DE L'ONTARIO

Design by Darrell McCalla
Printed in Hong Kong, China

Larger than Life

Tim Horton
From Stanley Cups to Coffee Cups

Don Quinlan

Fitzhenry & Whiteside

A very special thanks to the indefatigable
Christie Harkin for her passionate and professional dedication
to the successful completion of this project. Without her efforts,
this book would still be an idea, rather than a reality.

Thanks also to Richard McQuade, Director of Archives,
St. Michael's College School;
Aden Lannon; ECW Press; and Tim Donut Ltd.

Contents

Tim Horton: From Pucks to Donuts

**1ST TEAM ALL-STAR
TIM HORTON**

Tim Horton was one of Canada's greatest hockey players. In fact, he sits at number 43 on the Greatest 100 List compiled by *Hockey News*. He is certainly acknowledged by many fans and players alike to have been the strongest man ever to lace up skates. He earned awards and shared the joy of winning four Stanley Cups (including, as of 2009, the last one won by the famed Toronto Maple Leafs). Tim also founded a brilliantly successful chain of coffee shops that have come to represent Canada almost as much as the game of hockey itself.

Tim enjoyed playing hockey from the age of 5 until the night he died when he was 44 years old. His was a tough and bruising game. This is the story of that young boy who grew up to help build a hockey dynasty and a business empire.

Most people in Canada have heard of Tim Hortons. Kids of all ages think of a fabulous display of fresh donuts. Which ones to choose? The chocolate, the blueberry—or perhaps the ones with sprinkles?

Many probably see Tim Hortons as just another very successful fast food franchise. However, the story of Tim Horton is not really just about hot coffee and warm donuts. It begins, like many Canadian success stories, in the winter, on frozen ponds and arenas in a very Canadian northern landscape. And it begins with the story of a young boy on a pair of skates. He was strong—very strong—and he loved to play sports. Especially hockey.

Chapter One

A Northern Boy

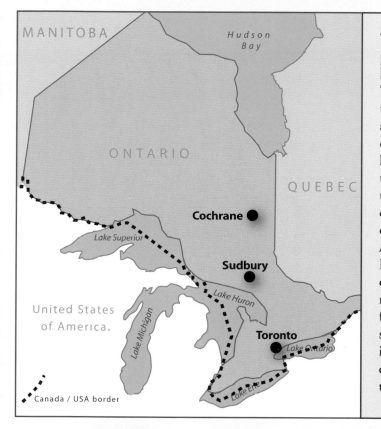

The Ontario northland has provided some very fine hockey players over the years. The isolation, the long winters, the numerous frozen ponds and lakes, and perhaps the demanding landscape and the heavy physical labor required to make a living in past days: these factors all worked to create a tough, persistent type of player. Tim Horton, George Armstrong, Eddie Shack, and Dave Keon were all examples of this kind of player from the north. Small towns often made for close communities where sports played an important role in bringing people together— especially before the days of television and the internet.

Tim Horton's childhood was tough. He remembered neighbors leaving charity food baskets on his family's doorstep. Hockey was his ticket out of a life of poverty in the hardscrabble north of Ontario.

Strangely, the famous "Tim" Horton was actually born Miles Gilbert Horton in the far north town of Cochrane, Ontario on January 12, 1930. Luckily, his mother, Ethel, preferred the name "Tim" to Miles and Gilbert (which were the names of his two grandfathers). Imagine going to Miles Gilbert Horton's for a donut and drink!

A Northern Family

Ontario's northland was much more isolated than it is today. It was home to mining towns and lumber towns. The railroad was a major connector of communities.

> "His mother told me he got a complete hockey outfit the Christmas he was six, and Tim always says that was the best Christmas he ever had."
>
> Lori Horton, Tim's wife, in
> *Remembering Tim Horton: A Celebration*

Although born in Cochrane, Ontario, Tim moved with the family to Duparquet, Quebec in 1936 for a few years, where Tim's father worked in a gold mine. It was here that the future hockey legend first laced up his skates on the frozen ponds and rivers of northern Quebec. Like many families, they moved from place to place in order to find work. Tim's father, Aaron Oakley Horton, known simply as "Oak", worked on the railways and in the mining camps. After two years in Duparquet, "Oak" brought the Horton family back to the Cochrane area in order to search for another job.

Tim continued to grow and gain strength. In Cochrane, Tim's hockey skills brought him much attention. In his

last game there, when he was fifteen years old, Tim led the local team to a mighty eight-goal victory. Remarkably, Tim scored all eight goals! Tired of travelling for work, Oak moved his family into the Sudbury region in 1945. Not only would Sudbury provide the family with roots and stability, but it was also the birth-place of some great hockey players and great competition. Sudbury hockey would change Tim's life.

The Copper Cliff Redmen

Hockey in the north was rough and tough. Sudbury was a hotbed of hockey activity with many capable play-ers. It was also undergoing a new age of prosperity, thanks to a "boom" in the mining industry. A mining boom meant lots of good-paying jobs for the local community. People could build a better future for their families. It also meant that the community could afford to build better facilities for its citizens—including a network of arenas that allowed players and fans to enjoy the sport indoors. In most remote communities, the ice rink was no more than a frozen pond or river. But with more money in their pockets, the people of Sudbury were happy to pay to see talented local players compete in a covered arena. Thus, the wealth in the ground helped the community to develop some of Canada's greatest hockey players—from the ground up.

> **"There wasn't much you could do in Cochrane, other than play hockey."**
>
> Gerry Horton, Tim's brother, in *Open Ice: The Tim Horton Story*

The Northern Mining Boom

Ontario's northland is home to vast deposits of such valuable minerals as copper, gold, silver, nickel, iron, and uranium. In the early 1900s, many mining communities were born in this once isolated region.

The need for metals for the production of war materials during the Second World War meant a huge economic boom in towns such as Sudbury and Copper Cliff. Towns and mining companies now had the money to build community projects like hockey arenas. It was in these small town arenas that some of Canada's greatest hockey players were developed.

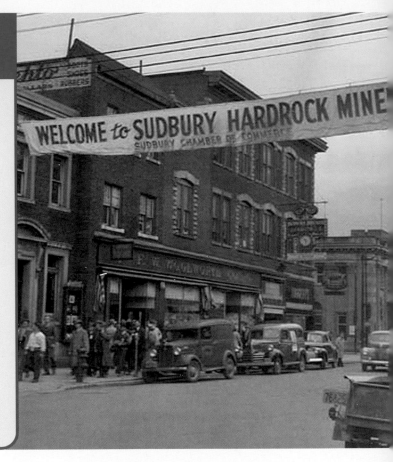

"Born into the depths of the Great Depression, hockey was more than just fun for Horton. It was a way out, an escape from his family's abject poverty."

CBC Life and Times

Competition was intense in the north, and soon NHL scouts put a northbound trip into their travel plans as they searched for the next superstar that might take their team to a Stanley Cup victory. In the late 1940s, being a teenager was not a barrier to signing with an NHL team. In fact, one of the problems for teachers and parents was that many kids simply quit school in order to take a shot at playing as professionals. Of course, few could make it into the six-team NHL of the time, and they risked their futures for an outside chance at fame and glory on the ice.

Though Tim was an avid athlete, he was not about to take that kind of a chance with his future. Tim was generally good at school, although it did not come easily to him. He was a fairly solid student with a B average in grades nine and ten. His parents also wanted him to finish high school. So Tim managed to make school and sports work together. But it made for a very busy, active lifestyle. A few days after finishing up the football season, hockey season opened. When Tim was in grade eleven, he played on his Sudbury high school hockey team at the same time as he was trying out for the local Junior A team, the Copper Cliff Redmen.

Without trips to the gym or self-improvement machines, Tim Horton developed a very powerful physique by simply being active and working hard at whatever task was at hand. Even at the age of 16 he displayed a lean, muscular body. His strength was one of his hallmarks as a player and probably helped extend his career.

It was while he was playing for the Copper Cliff Redmen that Tim began to develop into a future Hall of Fame defenseman. He could skate and he could score like a forward, but his sheer strength made him a good choice as a stay-at-home defenseman. This role meant that he could use his strength to protect his goalie and drive opposing players away from the net, rather than worry about making plays that would help his team score goals. Tim's first season for the Redmen (1946-47) was somewhat unremarkable, but it was important as a learning experience. He scored no points during the season. His tendency to take penalties sometimes hurt his team. In the rough playoff season, Tim's strength was a major asset to his team, which was loaded with scorers but not a lot of players with Tim's physical abilities.

In 1946, Tim suffered what could have been a career-ending injury when he fractured his cheekbone in a high-school game. It was a pretty serious injury, but he managed to battle back from it. Some observers feel that this incident might have weakened his eyesight, but Tim's eyesight had always been simply dreadful—he was almost blind in one eye. In fact, Tim often did his math homework with his head pressed to the table so that he could see the numbers and symbols. It was a physical defect that he learned to overcome throughout his sports career. There were no contact lenses in those early days. Off the ice, Tim looked like Mr. Magoo of the famous cartoon and wore very thick, coke-bottle glasses.

Unfortunately, even though he was able to return to the ice after that first accident, Tim was still forced to end his first and only season with the Redmen early, after a heavy crash into the boards resulted in a broken ankle.

Opportunity!

One of Tim's teammates on both his Redmen and high-school teams was the future Hall-of-Famer, George Armstrong. Armstrong was already a local legend who had been keen to take his game to the NHL. The Toronto Maple Leafs tried to get him to move south to play for the famous St. Michael's College School Majors hockey team. But Armstrong had already quit school before completing grade eleven in order to play for the Stratford Kroehlers in the Ontario Hockey League. As a result, Armstrong was unable to enter grade twelve at St. Michael's. The position on the Majors was then offered to Tim, who was willing to continue his studies and play hockey at the same time. Tim left the north forever to build a career in the south. It was a big move and a bit of a gamble for Tim and for St. Mike's. Ultimately, it was a gamble that paid huge results for both.

George Armstrong, future captain of the Toronto Maple Leafs

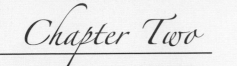

Chapter Two

"St. Mike's"

The original site of St. Michael's College School, home of the St. Mike's Majors.

Going to "St. Mike's" was a huge step for a young hockey player from northern Ontario. St. Michael's College School is a high school run by Catholic priests. It emphasizes academics and physical fitness. The school is located in Toronto, a gigantic city to a kid from smaller towns in Ontario and Quebec. Tim was a complete stranger to the city and to his classmates. Receiving a prized sports scholarship to such a hotbed of sports and academic excellence was one sure way out of a world of physical labor in the mines or pulp mills of the north. For many young men, the change and the challenge might have been a disaster, but Tim made the most of this marvelous opportunity. Interestingly, although the school is a celebrated Catholic institution, Tim was Protestant and was excused from religion classes; however, he continued to practice his faith on his own.

The St. Michael's College School and its hockey team have a reputation for being a breeding ground for greatness. Future Maple Leafs stars such as Ted Lindsay, Frank Mahovlich, Dick Duff, and the great Dave Keon attended the institution. Over 170 St. Mike's Majors have gone on to enter the NHL: Eventually, 13 of those would be inducted into the Hockey Hall of Fame. In 2006, St. Mike's celebrated its 100th year of hockey.

In 1947, however, Tim arrived as the team was beginning a long, downward slide. Nearly all of its previously successful team members had left to further their education or to play pro hockey. Thus the Majors were in rebuilding mode: They needed help, and Tim was ready to provide all that he could. This was the perfect opportunity for Tim to

TIM HAS BEEN A STAR ON THE MAJORS DEFENSE FOR TWO SEASONS.

TIM PLAYED MINOR HOCKEY IN COPPER CLIFF BEFORE COMING TO ST. MICHAEL'S

TIM HORTON

COPPER CLIFF JOE HALLORAN '??

TORONTO

CHOSEN ~ THE BEST DEFENSEMAN IN THE JUNIOR "A" OHA DURING 1948-49.

Tim was soon popular at St. Mike's and was noted in his school yearbook. He was known as "Tim the Terrible."

grow as a player. He was getting bigger and stronger—he even did push-ups at the end of his bed and chin-ups on the shower rod in his bathroom. Tim was much tougher than the other players, and he threw his weight and strength around more aggressively. He earned more penalty minutes in the 1947-48 season than any other player in the OHA—with 137 minutes or a 4.28 minute-average per game—but these were not the result of dirty play. Tim was simply a tough player—not a hockey "goon." His job was to clear the ice of opposing players, and he did this very well. He also began to develop more as a rushing defenseman who could create scoring

Although Tim did not stay long at St. Mike's (two years), he made a solid impact and was chosen as the Ontario Hockey Association's (OHA) best defenseman in his first season (1948-49). Tim is on the far left, wearing number 3.

opportunities, rather than simply being a stay-at-home type of player. Although the team was not very successful and Tim didn't score lots of goals, he was winning recognition for his toughness, speed, and heart. He always tried hard to keep the Majors competitive in every game. At the end of that first losing season, his fellow players honored their star defenseman by voting him their team MVP.

Schoolwork

Being both a hockey player and a student was hard. Players had early morning practices, afternoon practices, and of course, games. Playing on the school hockey team sometimes meant missing classes. Students were expected to make up the work on their own and to keep track of homework assignments. Tim was not a gifted student and school was not easy for him, but he did apply himself. His legendary poor eyesight made some assignments difficult to do. Tim did not earn all his credits that first year, so he returned to St. Mike's for another year. The team was glad to have him available again. The Majors still struggled, but the reputation of its star player only grew. At the end of Tim's second season, those who knew his worth the most—his fellow players—named him their MVP once again. Then, as Tim looked to return for one more season and get his last high school credit, things changed forever.

> **"Tim was the star of the team. People used to go to the games just to watch him. They loved him.'"**
>
> Dick Trainor in *Open Ice*

In September 1949, Tim received the call to attend the Maple Leafs hockey school in St. Catharines, Ontario.

It was another important opportunity and, as in the past, he made the most of it.

Turning Pro

In 1949, Tim made a life-changing decision and joined the Pittsburgh Hornets (a Leafs farm team) for a salary of $3000 a year. This was more than he could make in most other occupations but, in relative terms, it was not the princely sum that hockey players can earn today. Still, it was enough to make a huge difference, not only in his professional career but in his personal life, too. As soon as Tim had his money, he went out and bought himself a car—a 1949 Mercury. Tim felt that he had truly arrived.

Part of being on a hockey team can include traveling on a bus and dressing up for games. Tim is the fellow in the middle with the funny hat.

Chapter Three

Hockey and Marriage

Tim's rough–and-ready style of play was one of the key ingredients in the success of the Pittsburgh Hornets. His star quality also caused his future wife, Lori, to take note of the young player.

Pittsburgh

Tim's professional hockey career began in the fall of 1949 when he started his three-year contract with the Pittsburgh Hornets of the American Hockey League (AHL). In those days, the Hornets were considered a Maple Leafs "farm team," meaning that the Leafs often looked to the Hornets as a source of talented new players. Over those three years, Tim matured rapidly as a hockey player and a person, hoping for a chance to move up to the big leagues of the NHL. In one memorable exhibition game with the Maple Leafs, Tim thrilled Hornets fans and alerted the Leafs to his growing talent. He set up goals and battled and bumped all of the major Leafs players. Tim was letting them know that he was NHL material. One sports writer noted that Tim, a "fast-travelling, hard-hitting youngster who hardly has had time to dry the ink on his professional hockey contract served notice here tonight that he rates serious consideration for a major-league post in the near future." With only six teams in the NHL, the minor leagues would make or break careers for thousands of young hockey players. It was important to work hard, stay healthy, and get noticed. Tim did just that.

The AHL

The American Hockey League was born out of the merger of the Canadian-American Hockey League and the International Hockey League in 1936, forming the International-American Hockey League (the "International" was removed from the name in 1940). All teams were American until 1959 when the Quebec Aces joined the league. Many AHL teams are linked to NHL teams and serve as training grounds for future stars of the NHL. By 2009, there were 29 teams in the AHL, with 3 of them being Canadian.

King Clancy
(1903-1986)

Francis Michael "King" Clancy was one of the most colorful figures in hockey. He started his playing career with the Ottawa Senators in 1921, using hand-me-down skates. He was only 17 years old. In one memorable game, Clancy played all six positions! He joined the Toronto Maple Leafs in 1930. After a brilliant playing career, he moved on to coaching and refereeing in the NHL. He later served as assistant general manager of the Leafs from 1956 until his death in 1986. One of the game's best-liked characters, he was inducted into the Hockey Hall of Fame in 1958. Today, the **King Clancy Memorial Trophy** is awarded annually to the NHL player who best exemplifies leadership qualities on and off the ice and who has made a significant humanitarian contribution in his community.

He learned his craft well. He practiced and played hard. At the end of his first season with Pittsburgh, the Leafs called him up to play one game. However, he only had enough time to get a penalty before returning to Pittsburgh for another season. During his time in Pittsburg, Tim was fortunate to have had two coaches who helped him develop as a top player— Joe Primeau and King Clancy. Tim also began to cultivate one of the best slapshots in professional hockey. It was a tool that would win him much admiration and recognition. Speed, a great shot, strength, and toughness—Tim had everything a future Hall-of-Famer would need.

Tim and the Hornets improved steadily. In his second season (1950-51), the Hornets made the AHL finals, only losing in the very last game of the championship series. By his third season (1951-52), the team was a major force in the AHL. In 1952, Tim and the Hornets won the Calder Cup— Pittsburgh's first-ever championship. Tim was also named an American League All-Star in the same year.

The Flaw

In spite of Tim's superb physique and devotion to hard work and exercise, he did have one serious flaw that continued to nag him throughout his long career: His eyesight was terrible. In fact, it is somewhat miraculous that he was able to play such a fast-moving sport where hand-to-eye coordination is so vital. But Tim had an instinct for the game and could sense where the puck was likely to be. This strong hockey sense helped Tim to compensate for his weak eyesight. At times when he was younger, Tim was accused of hogging the puck, but friends claim that he simply could not see clearly enough to pass the puck; it was safer for him to hold on to it and simply hammer his way forward—often directly over opposing players.

Tim spent most of his star-studded career suffering from weak eyesight. He learned to cope rather than let this weakness end his hockey dreams. This is what he looked like when not in uniform.

Throughout his career, he would make special arrangements with teammates so that his eyesight would not interfere with other aspects of his game. For example, other players knew that they should send the puck just in front of him on a pass. They would also call out to him for a pass so that he knew where they were and if they were open.

When Tim joined the Pittsburgh Hornets, the team management did something practical to help their new team member; their optometrist created a special type of heavy-duty contact lens that Tim used for several years. Although awkward and uncomfortable, he could actually see. Off the ice, Tim now wore some very dark and heavy horn-rimmed glasses with lenses so large that they looked like fishbowls. He earned the name Mr. Magoo for wearing them. During his career, he was also called Cousin Weak-Eyes by his teammates.

One can only imagine how Tim's career might have developed if the wonder of modern laser-eye surgery had been available to him. Nevertheless, Tim is an example of how people can overcome certain flaws to achieve greatness in their chosen fields. He had strength of character to complement his abundant physical strength.

Lori

Tim's eyes may have been weak, but they were always good for spotting a pretty girl. Lori Michalek was an excellent skater herself, and she often skated at the same Pittsburgh rink where the Hornets played. Lori had taken notice of Tim and had even cut out his picture from a hockey program. They were introduced by a common friend and soon their romance was on. Tim proposed and they married in 1952 at the end of the Hornets' season, after moving the date at least once— because of a hockey game! They had a brief honeymoon in Florida before Tim took Lori to a cottage near North Bay and introduced her to her new family and a new country—Canada.

The Horton family (and pet) in 1955: Tim, baby Kim, Lori, and Jeri-Lynn

Tim and Lori would stay together through thick and
thin, through the good times and some very bad times.
They raised four beautiful girls whom they adored. They
were relatively poor and then relatively rich. Although
their marriage faced some big challenges, it was the only
one for both of them.

A Different Kind of Hockey

Unlike today, coaches did not generally control every aspect of the game. The players were responsible for motivating themselves, and they even suggested strategies and improvements for team play. As a player gained experience, he naturally took on a bigger role in the development of the team. Since players did not move around as much from team to team as they do today, real lasting friendships and true team spirit developed. This could mean crazy hi-jinks, but it also meant that everyone held greater responsibility for the team's fortunes.

The NHL Calls

At the end of the Hornets' victorious 1952 season, Tim was called up to attend his third Toronto Maple Leafs rookie training camp. It was to be his last. He made the team and began an NHL career of 23 seasons—a full 19 with the Leafs. Tim would never retire from the NHL.

"One day Anderson (the Pittsburgh coach) called a special meeting. He told us it had become obvious that we didn't want to listen to him and that we might as well pick our own lines and defensive pairings for the remaining six games and that he would only open and close the gate. We agreed. We picked the lineup and let him know before each game. All he did was send out the line as we selected them. We won the last five games and made it into the playoffs."

Tim Horton in
Remembering Tim Horton

Chapter Four

The Leafs

The Mystery

Sometimes in life, one person has to leave before another gets an opportunity to join in. Tim had won a chance to go to St. Mike's because George Armstrong had left school in order to focus on his hockey career. Tim's entry to the fabled Toronto Maple Leafs began with the same kind of chance event. One of the Leafs' greatest players was defenseman "Bashing" Bill Barilko, another rugged northerner, from Timmins, Ontario. In 1951, Barilko was at the top of his game and his fame.

The famous last goal of Bill Barilko's life. It was also the goal that won the Leafs their last Stanley Cup until 1962.

During his five seasons with the Leafs, Barilko participated in four Stanley Cup championships. Early in 1951, Barilko scored an overtime goal that gave the Leafs the Stanley Cup. Toronto was mad for the young, bruising-type hockey player. However, in the summer of 1951, Barilko went on a fishing trip—but his plane never returned. Barilko and his friends simply disappeared from sight. The tragic disappearance of Bill Barilko unleashed one of the greatest mysteries in professional hockey. It gripped the imagination of fans all across Canada and was the subject of rumors and wild theories.

For the Toronto Maple Leafs, the mystery of Barilko became somewhat of a curse. The team did not win another Stanley Cup for 11 years—not until 1962 when the doomed plane's wreckage was finally spotted near Cochrane, Ontario, the birthplace of Tim Horton. The discovery of the plane seemed to bring an end to the gloomy years of the team, and they soon embarked on another run of glory in the 1960s. In the meantime, the tragic loss of Barilko in 1951 had created an opening for a player on the Maple Leafs, and Tim was called up from the Hornets to fill that gap.

The First NHL Years

Unfortunately for Tim, his NHL arrival as a member of one of its most storied teams coincided with the end of a great period of victorious play for the Leafs. All teams have ups and downs, as Tim had learned when he first went to play with the struggling St. Mike's Majors. Like the Majors, the Leafs were in a rebuilding period when Tim arrived in 1951, and he did not see the glory years of the team for over a decade. However, the NHL was still the big-time, and Tim soon showed the promise that the Leafs were to rely on for nearly 20 years.

As before, Tim continued to grow as a hockey player, gaining strength and speed. He was sometimes called the "Pony Express" because he would take the puck and tear down the ice, daring anyone to stop him. His slapshot became stronger and more accurate. He faced some frustration too. He liked to rush down the ice and be part of the scoring, but often his coaches wanted him to stay in his own end of the ice and protect the goal. Tim was able to do both but missed being able to score the way he did as a younger player.

A Growing Family

While he was growing as a professional hockey player, Tim also had mounting responsibilities at home. Within eight years, he and Lori had four daughters. The first, Jeri-Lynn, was born in 1952. The others followed quickly: Kim in 1955, Kelly in 1956, and finally Traci in 1959. Even though Tim was a professional hockey player with one of the greatest teams in the league, he did not earn the kind of wealth that many professional

Tim Horton's hockey card from 1955-56

Tim and Lori were soon parents of four very attractive and lively young girls. Working away from his family so much added challenges to Tim and Lori's life.

athletes earn today. Hockey players drew a decent salary in the '50s and '60s, but it was nothing compared to the million dollar salaries even an average player can demand today. So, raising a family, finding a new house, and balancing career and personal responsibilities became distracting problems for most professional hockey players. Tim spent many days and nights far from his family when he was on the road in the NHL. Then, in the summer, he often had to find additional work, resulting in more time away from the girls, whom he clearly loved. This back-and-forth lifestyle meant that much more of the family responsibilities fell to Lori, his young wife.

Making a Living in the Off-Season

Like so many other players, Tim worked hard during the off-season: Over his career, he carried bricks and even fought forest fires. At one point, he worked for the Maple Leafs' owner in the summer, driving a gravel truck.

It was Tim's natural energy, solid work habits, and the need to provide for his growing family that led him into a series of business ventures, many of which didn't really work out that well. He started a hamburger shop with his brother Gerry in North Bay, but that meant long drives almost every weekend to tend to the business. Another time, he worked for Brewer's Retail (the Beer Store) and for the *Toronto Star* before trying his hand as a real estate agent. The search for more money was a constant in his life.

The Off-Season

When Tim was starting his career, most hockey players received a modest salary and found work doing anything and everything, from physical labour to driving cabs. Today, players earn huge salaries, many in the millions of dollars. Few have to take summer jobs, but many remain active by running or teaching hockey schools. Some participate in charity fundraising efforts such as golfing or biking events. Often players stay fit by maintaining a personal training regime or practicing summer sports such as soccer or baseball. A few go to summer school to prepare for a post-hockey career, often in business or broadcasting.

The Injury

Tim was one of the toughest players ever to hit the ice in the NHL, and he was one of the game's most durable "ironmen." He played a tough and clean but rough-and-tumble physical game. He was often bruised and scarred, but he rarely missed a game due to illness or injury. Near the end of the 1955-56 season, however, one terrible bodycheck in a game against the New York Rangers changed all that. For some players, it could have been a career-ending injury.

Tim was one of the toughest players ever to play the game of hockey, but even he received career-threatening injuries.

As Tim was rushing down the ice, he appeared to momentarily lose sight of the puck (Remember the poor eyesight!). He put his head down for a moment—perhaps the most dangerous thing a hockey player can do—and was hit with a bone-crushing, but clean, bodycheck from another hard-hitting player, Bill Gadsby. The entire rink apparently heard the snapping of his leg as the two players collided. Tim was on the ice in considerable pain. He not only had broken his leg, but he also had fractured his jaw. Gadsby later declared that it was the hardest hit he had ever delivered and he was genuinely sorry for the devastating impact of his check.

Tim's leg was in a cast and his jaw was wired. His doctors marveled at how little he complained and how quickly he mended. His doctor noted, "He must have been suffering terrible pain, but there wasn't a peep out of him," (Dr. Hugh Smythe in *Remembering Tim Horton*.)

What did hurt Tim, however, was the treatment he received from the Leafs organization for which he had worked so hard. The Leafs lowered his salary to make up for the time he missed. Then, since he was slow to get back to his peak form in the next season, they fined him. Once again, Tim learned that he could not simply rely on hockey to provide a proper income for his family.

A Brighter Future

The "frustrating fifties" began to change for the Leafs near the end of the decade. Rookies like Tim Horton were now seasoned veterans, and new players were being acquired to build the basis for a great team. For Tim, the 1958 arrival of another northerner, defenseman Allan "Snowshoe" Stanley, created a pairing of two great defensive stars that would anchor the Leafs throughout the coming glory years of the '60s. Another key change was the naming of George "Punch" Imlach as general manager and head coach in the same year. Slowly but surely, the Toronto Maple Leafs were putting the pieces together for an exciting future.

Chapter Five
The Great Years

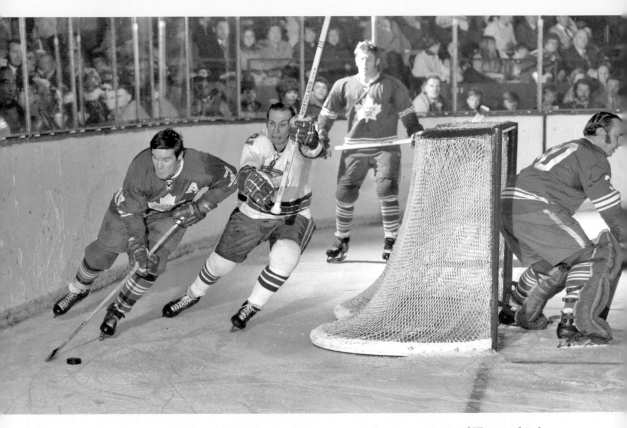

For many people, this shot of Tim in action represents their memories of Tim at his best—strong, alert, and whole-heartedly involved in the great Canadian game of hockey.

ince the mysterious disappearance of "Bashing" Bill Barilko, the Toronto Maple Leafs had been a team in decline. During Barilko's four-and-one-half years in the NHL, the Leafs had won the Stanley Cup four times. After his disappearance, the team went Cupless for eleven straight seasons. To the superstitious, it seemed that the loss of Barilko had unleashed some sort of curse on the team. Fans talked of the "ghost of Barilko." Finally, in 1962, the mystery was solved when Barilko's float plane was discovered. With the ghost settled and the supposed curse lifted, the Leafs won another Stanley Cup that same year—in large part thanks to the hard work of the man who replaced him: Tim Horton.

The Golden Age

The Toronto Maple Leafs' glory years of the early 1960s were built on the foundation of one of the greatest teams in professional hockey. Its players quickly became household names. Many were elected later to the Hockey Hall of Fame; most lived to be lovingly celebrated by Toronto hockey fans in a moving and enthusiastic tribute celebration in 2007.

Any good team needs excellent defense. If the other team cannot score, it is more likely that your team will win. To keep pucks out of the net, you need solid goaltending: In this respect, the Leafs enjoyed the work of aging veterans such as Johnny Bower and Terry Sawchuck, who were often spectacular in net. Joining the stellar line of Tim Horton and Allan Stanley on defense was the equally effective pair of Bobby Baun and Carl Brewer. Bobby Baun earned legendary status during the 1964 Stanley Cup finals, when he stayed on the ice with a broken ankle and scored the winning goal during overtime against the Detroit Red Wings.

Terry Sawchuk was one of the famous "over-the-hill gang" that helped lead the Leafs to Stanley Cup glory in 1967. He was a tough goalie who received more than 400 stitches to his face over his long career.

The Leafs of the 1960s could score goals—lots of goals. Their forwards included the scoring geniuses of Dave Keon, Frank Mahovlich, Dick Duff, and Bob Pulford. The brilliant playmaker Red Kelly had also come over from Detroit and switched from defense to forward. Tim's former northern teammate, George "Chief" Armstrong, provided all-important leadership as captain. Defense, scoring, and leadership: just what the Leafs needed to move from the frustration of the fifties to the success of the sixties.

Rivalry: Leafs vs Habs

The Toronto-Montreal rivalry exists not only between two of the Original Six hockey teams, but it often involves the citizens of the respective cities. The battle to be better than the other stretches back to the early years of the NHL and continues to this very day, although recently both teams have ceased to be true NHL powerhouses. Still, it has resulted in some of the most magnificent hockey ever played. As of 2009, Montreal has won the most Stanley Cups (24) and Toronto has come second with 13. Even today when the teams meet on the ice, the sold-out games still tend to be intense, leaving their fans hoarse from cheering (or booing).

A Tale of Two Cities

One of the greatest sports rivalries of all times exists between the Montreal Canadiens and the Toronto Maple Leafs. Both vie to be Canada's team. Both cities want to be Canada's greatest. In the 1950s, while the Leafs lagged behind,

Ellis Robbed By Habs

Here, Ron Ellis tries to break through the Habs wall of Jacques Laperriere, J.C. Tremblay, Henri Richard, and goalie Charlie Hodge.

Montreal made the finals every year, winning six times (including a record five straight between 1956 and 1960). To some, these teams of the 1950s were the greatest in hockey history. The Montreal powerhouse was led by the incredible Maurice "Rocket" Richard, his younger brother Henri "the Pocket Rocket" Richard, Jean Beliveau, Bernie "Boom Boom" Geoffrion, Jacques Plante, and Doug Harvey.

However, as the 1950s wound down, Toronto began to creep up in the standings and squeeze into the playoffs.

"These are the games. Oh boy-oh-boy, one half of the country against the other— everybody watching. I can't describe the feeling—you feel like you've spent your whole life preparing for this night."

Terry Harper in *Hockey: A People's History*

When the great "Rocket" Richard retired in 1960, Montreal hoped to continue winning, but they faltered. Toronto soon became the next powerhouse in the NHL. In 1962 a re-energized Toronto muscled past their great rival and made it to the finals. There, they defeated the Chicago Blackhawks and proudly paraded the Stanley Cup through the streets of Toronto once again. Tim Horton played a central role in that victory, setting a record for the time by scoring three goals and thirteen assists. In fact, it was Tim's rush up the ice and pin-point pass to Dick Duff that led to the Stanley Cup–winning goal!

The First Cup is the Sweetest

In 1962, the Leafs' return to the Stanley Cup champion-ship started yet another period of great hockey. The nucleus of a legendary team took shape. For some observers, the early '60s represent a Golden Age of

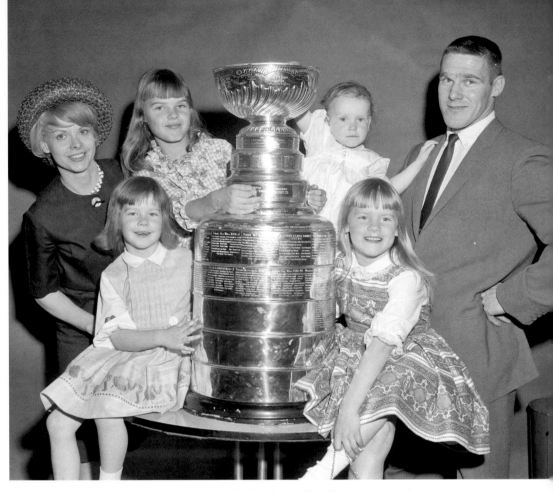

The Horton family celebrates a Maple Leafs Stanley Cup victory.

hockey for the NHL. For the Leafs, the period from 1962-64 meant three Stanley Cups in a row, and Tim Horton was a key member of those memorable teams.

The 1960s were good to Toronto and to Tim. Together they achieved great success. Tim matured into one of the steadiest defenders in hockey. He was the reliable anchor of some great Leafs teams. Tim was voted to the NHL First All-Star Team in 1964, 1968, and 1969. He was also selected to the NHL Second All-Star Team in 1963 and 1967. It was during this period that he built up his record of starting in 1446 NHL games. The record stood until 1996.

More remarkably, between February 11, 1961 and February 4, 1968, Horton played in 486 consecutive regular-season games; this is still the Leafs' club record for consecutive games and was the NHL record for consecutive games by a defenseman until it was broken by Karlis Skrastins of the Colorado Avalanche on February 8, 2007.

> **"I would say that Horton, a little more than any other player, was the key to the success we had. He was always there, always the same, always giving the effort, the best he had every night."**
>
> Punch Imlach in *Remembering Tim Horton*

Hockey Night in Canada

One of the most popular shows in Canada for decades has been *Hockey Night in Canada* (*HNIC*). It started on a network of radio stations in 1933. *HNIC* became a national Canadian Broadcasting Corporation (CBC) television institution in 1952, when broadcaster Foster Hewitt welcomed the country to the game with his famous "Hello, Canada!" By 2007, its *Coach's Corner* segment with Don Cherry had become the highest rated television spot in Canada.

In 1995, *HNIC* first broadcast a two-game double-header on Saturday night: one in the east and one in the west. The famous theme music (now adopted by The Sports Network for their hockey broadcasts) was written by Dolores Claman in 1968 and is sometimes referred to as Canada's "second national anthem." The first radio games were broadcast for $100 a game. By 2007, the rights to

*For most Canadians, Foster Hewitt was the "voice of hockey" for decades. The **Foster Hewitt Memorial Award** for broadcasting, given by the Hockey Hall of Fame, is named in his honor.*

broadcast NHL games had risen to an astronomical $65 million a season.

The great Toronto-Montreal rivalry soon became part of Canada's national identity. In the 1960s, television began to change the game. Before the advent of commercial television, fans only had the radio or newspapers. Even young players like Tim Horton could not see their heroes play or even try to copy their moves. By 1967, however, televisions were in nearly 90% of

Canadian homes. Now, every child could enjoy and learn from the playmaking of a Tim Horton or the scoring of a Dave Keon. Fans could actually see and hear every play.

The Canadian love of hockey united the country in a way that it never had been before. All Canadians knew the famous phrase, "He shoots! He scores!"

The advent of television brought the excitement of professional hockey into homes across North America.

Now they could see it happen. Television would increase the popularity of the game, expand the number of NHL teams, and bring vastly increased salaries to players and coaches. Hockey was definitely big time now.

The Donut Empire

In the midst of the excitement of the Maple Leafs victories and the three consecutive Stanley Cups from 1962-64, Tim Horton made yet another decision which would change his entire life. He was still working summers and

It was from such humble beginnings in a working-area part of Hamilton that the mighty Tim Hortons Donut empire was built.

trying to ensure a good enough income to raise his family and provide for his future. He had run a car dealership and a hamburger shop. He had worked at driving trucks and even selling homes. He was always willing to roll up his shirtsleeves and try something new. It is unlikely that he ever imagined that his future, fortune, and eventual fame would be found in donuts. In 1964, he met Dennis Griggs and Jim Charade, who were trying to open donut shops. They formed a company called Tim Donut Ltd. The idea was to attract customers by using Tim's popularity. The first Tim Horton Donuts was opened in Hamilton in 1964. In the early months, the first two or three stores faced difficulties. Eventually in 1965, Dennis and Jim left and sold their shares to Tim. Later that year, a retired police officer, Ron Joyce, joined Tim and Lori in the project. By 1967, after opening two more stores, Ron and Tim became full partners. In 1964, you could buy a dozen donuts for 69 cents and a cup of coffee for a mere quarter! Thus, a donut empire was born.

Chapter Six

The Over-the-Hill Gang

The Team

In 1967, Canada wildly celebrated its Centennial and Toronto wildly celebrated its last Stanley Cup victory (at least as of 2009), although it did not know it at the time. All across the country, local communities were creating special Centennial projects. One of the most popular projects was to build a new "Centennial" hockey arena. At 100, Canada was still a relatively young country in the world; however, many Maple Leafs players were quite old, by professional hockey player standards.

For most people, hockey is a young person's game. It requires great speed, strength, and endurance. Athletes tend to hit their peaks in their late 20s and early 30s. While age does bring experience, few winning teams are built around a core group of much older players. In fact, players over thirty-five years old are often thought to be past their prime. Some people use the expression "over the hill" to describe these older players.

Although the Maple Leafs had tasted three consecutive Stanley Cup victories, 1965 marked the beginning of a minor slump. In an attempt to shake things up, coach Punch Imlach tried moving Tim from his usual position on defense to right wing! For part of a season, Tim found himself on a forward line with George Armstrong and Red Kelly, another former defenseman. As a winger, Tim used his big slapshot to his advantage: instead of firing the puck on net from the blue line, he was able to blast it in from close range. Many of his 12 goals that season were scored in this manner. But for the two seasons from 1964-1966, it wasn't enough. The Leafs did not even make the finals in those years.

To make matters worse, they had been beaten in the semi-finals by none other than their arch rivals, the Montreal Canadiens. While the Leafs were faltering, the Canadiens had returned to their winning ways. They regained the Stanley Cup in both the 1964-65 and 1965-66 seasons. In the last semi-final in 1966, Montreal

> **"What people forget is he (Tim) had one of the first big slap-shots. That way of shooting the puck started in the late '50s when Bobby Hull became a star. But Tim was already doing it, hammering those boomers from the point."**
>
> Allan Stanley in *Remembering Tim Horton*

hammered the Leafs, winning the best-of-seven series in four straight games. The future did not look bright for the Leafs, and a new period of rebuilding seemed near.

The Toronto Maple Leafs of the 1966-67 NHL season represent hockey's oldest team to win the Stanley Cup. It was a most unexpected victory from a most unexpected group of players. Of course, one of the key elements in that remarkable march to victory was 37–year-old Tim Horton, who still had quite a few eventful years of hockey in his aging body.

Along with Tim, the Leafs had ten players over thirty including the following players: 42-year-old goalie, Johnny Bower; 41-year-old defenseman, Allan Stanley; 39-year-old forward, Red Kelly; 37-year-old goalie, Terry Sawchuck; and 36-year-old captain, George Armstrong. They were viewed as a group of "aging hardheads" from whom not much was to be expected. The over-the-hill gang proved them all wrong.

Stanley and Bower were inspirational living proof that hockey was not just a young person's game. In 1967, they skated into hockey history.

The Season

Certainly the regular NHL season did not suggest that this rapidly aging team was going anywhere. By mid-season, the Leafs appeared to be out of the playoffs. In fact in one terrible streak, they lost ten games straight. The fans were restless. Under all that pressure, Punch Imlach collapsed due to stress and was hospitalized. The Leafs finished strong, however, and squeaked into the playoffs. In the first round, they upset the Chicago Blackhawks in six games.

> **"Toronto was now very much a spent force. It was no longer a veteran team, it was just old."**
>
> Doug Herod in *Remembering Tim Horton: A Celebration*

The Stanley Cup Finals

The 1967 Stanley Cup playoffs held special significance for two reasons. First, it was Canada's hundredth birthday, and the finals would feature two rival Canadian teams: Toronto and Montreal. Second, these would be the last-ever playoffs featuring the NHL's Original Six teams. The Chicago Black Hawks, New York Rangers, Boston Bruins, Detroit Red Wings, Montreal Canadiens, and Toronto Maple Leafs would soon be overshadowed somewhat by successive waves of expansion teams. However, these six founding teams still hold a special place in an ever-expanding NHL that would eventually number thirty teams.

It was no secret that Montreal hoped to display the Stanley Cup in their city during Expo '67, when the world was invited to come and discover Canada during its Centennial year. The Canadiens' coach had promised the mayor of Montreal his team would bring the Stanley Cup home—and then display it in the Montreal pavilion during the World's Fair for all to see.

The stakes were high as Tim and his teammates moved on to the finals for this historic Centennial-year showdown with the Montreal Canadiens. Few expected that the Leafs, who had limped into the playoffs, would be much of a challenge for the younger, speedier Montreal players. The long Chicago series had left the aging Leafs bruised and battered, while Montreal had won its series against New York quickly in four straight games.

As predicted by some observers, the Leafs were blown out in the first game by a score of 6-2. Tim was on the ice for four of the Montreal goals—not a good statistic for a defenseman. In the second game, brilliant goaltending by Johnny Bower and a timely goal by Tim resulted in a 3-0 upset victory by the Leafs. They went on to claim Game 3 in a thrilling 3-2 overtime win. Bower stopped 52 of 54 shots.

In Game 4, however, the desperate Canadiens powered back to a crushing 6-2 victory over the Leafs. Heading into the next game, Tim and the other Leafs knew that they had to keep the other team out of their zone if they hoped to win. Their tough defensive lines bumped and wore down the flashier Montreal forwards before they could penetrate the Toronto zone. Tim not only contributed defensively—he also added some offence and scored another goal as the Leafs rallied to win 4-1.

In the final game of the last Original Six Stanley Cup Finals, coach Punch Imlach put the fate of the team in the hands of his over-the-hill gang. With the score close at 2-1, he lined up his aging veterans, Allan Stanley, Tim Horton, and Red Kelly in front of goaltender Johnny Bower in the last 55 seconds of play, for one of the last face-offs of the 1967 season. It was a mark of confidence in his older players—and it was the end of an era. Montreal pulled its goalie for an extra attacker. Moments later George Armstrong, 36, scored an empty-net goal to clinch the game and win the series.

The 1967 Toronto Maple Leafs – Stanley Cup Champions.

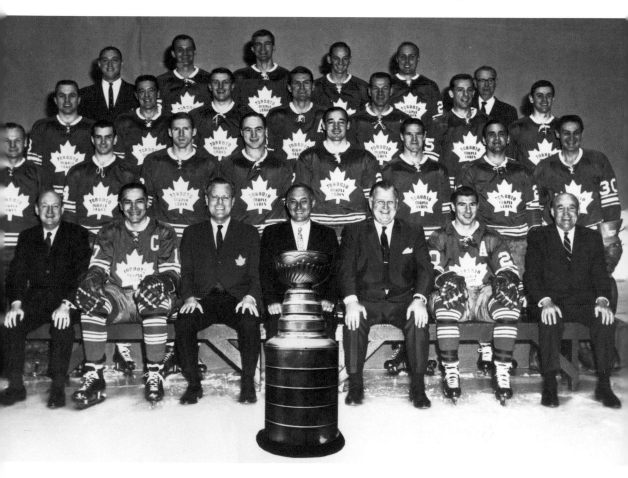

Against all odds, the "aging hardheads" had won the Stanley Cup one last time. It was a magical moment that Tim, the team, and their fans would treasure for years to come. Soon many of the players would be traded or retired. Toronto and Montreal have never played together in the Stanley Cup finals since. For some fans, a golden age of hockey history closed forever.

> "In the 67 playoffs, we let Punch talk to the media and run the bench because he was the master of both jobs. But to call him the coach of that team wasn't right. Guys like Tim Horton and George Armstrong and Red Kelly really called the shots on how we would try to handle the other teams."
>
> Unnamed Leaf veteran in *Remembering Tim Horton: A Celebration*

A Legendary Team

As of the 2008-09 season, Toronto has not won another Stanley Cup. The poor fans of Toronto have elevated that '67 team to almost legendary status. In February 2007, the Maple Leafs held a special tribute for the team and assembled the remaining players, now truly old, at the Maple Leafs' new home at the Air Canada Centre in Toronto. The elderly players, including George Armstrong, Bobby Baun, Johnny Bower, Ron Ellis, Red Kelly, Dave Keon, Jim Pappin, Eddie Shack, and Allan Stanley were treated to a huge outpouring of love and affection. It was a special night for all. Sadly, one of the greatest and most committed members of that team—Tim Horton—was not there.

Chapter Seven

After the Leafs

The New NHL

s the celebrating died down after the smashing Leafs victory in the Stanley Cup finals in the Centennial year, reality for the Leafs set in. The "aging hardheads" *were* older and they did

Tim helps his nine-year-old daughter, Tracey, with her school-work in the fall of 1969.

finally seem to be an "over-the-hill gang." Some players retired; others were traded away. At this point in his life and career, Tim began to think seriously about a life apart from hockey. While he had been battling his way through this extraordinary hockey season, his donut business had been expanding. He noted that "things are quite hectic these days—trying to combine business with hockey. And if the business that I am involved in continues as it is, I may have to consider retirement [from hockey] before I would like to." But Tim was wrong: he had a lot of hockey left in him yet.

> **"I didn't stay out of his reach. He put the bear hug on me and started to squeeze. I once read a news story on an earthquake where people heard the joist of their house start to groan and then crack. Well, in Horton's embrace, I heard my ribs groan and thought they were all going to crack. It really started to hurt, then he let me go and tossed me on my back like a towel. I never slashed him or challenged him again."**
>
> Derek Sanderson, former Boston Bruins centerman, in *Remembering Tim Horton*

Coach Punch Imlach was not popular with many of the players, although he and Tim always managed to work things out. Punch could be a very demanding taskmaster and some-times was verbally abusive toward his players. In 1969, Imlach was fired. Tim exclaimed, "If this team doesn't want Imlach, it doesn't want me." However, in the same year, the Leafs proved that they did indeed want Tim, since he was able to double his salary to a remarkable $90,000 a year. He also won the J.P. Bickell Memorial Cup, a team award for the Leafs' Most Valuable Player.

As a result of the newly expanded NHL, more players were needed to fill out the new rosters. Demand for veteran players of Tim's caliber was high. As well, the National

Hockey League Players' Association (NHLPA) was born in 1967, and players were working together to demand better wages, benefits, and working conditions. The old days of hockey were gone. Clearly, hockey had become a major business, and loyalty to teams and players was soon replaced by business principles and money.

So, with a growing donut chain and a higher salary, Tim seemed to have it made. However, the Leafs were moving in a new direction, and in 1970, the older, high-salaried defenseman was traded to the New York Rangers. Many fans were shocked to see a player leave who had been at the center of the Leafs for nearly twenty years. In fact, King Clancy cried when he learned that Tim was going.

Although Tim was older, he was still viewed as one of the strongest men in hockey. His conditioning was superb. He used weight training when few players and coaches did. As always, though he hit hard, Tim was considered a clean player. He did, however, defend his teammates. This fiercely protective spirit earned him the nickname "Tiger"

NHL Expansion

Throughout its long history, the NHL has expanded into more and more cities, giving communities across North America the chance to view world-class hockey in their own hometowns. Created in 1917, the NHL's first teams included the Montreal Canadiens, the Montreal Wanderers, the Ottawa Senators, the Quebec Bulldogs, and the Toronto Arenas (later the Maple Leafs). From 1942-67, the league membership was stable and composed of six teams. The "Original Six" include the Montreal Canadiens, Toronto Maple Leafs, Detroit Red Wings, Boston Bruins, New York Rangers and the Chicago Black Hawks. However, in 1967, the NHL rapidly expanded and doubled it size with new teams in American cities such as Pittsburgh, Los Angeles, Minnesota, Oakland, St. Louis, and Philadelphia. Over the next decades the NHL expanded and contracted depending on how the game was accepted in the towns with new NHL teams. Players increasingly were drawn from the U.S. and Europe as well as Canada. By 2007, the NHL had 30 teams scattered across North America from Toronto to Tampa and Vancouver to New York.

while he was with the Leafs. New York was hoping to win the Cup that year, and it felt that Tim, with his strength and veteran leadership, could help them do just that. When they fell short, he was sent to the Pittsburgh Penguins, a new expansion team now coached by his former teammate, Red Kelly. For Lori, it was a chance to go back home.

The Business

Tim and Ron Joyce were still busy building their dream business. They opened more and more donut shops: By 1974, there were 35 Tim Horton Donut locations. Tim

even helped in the construction of some of them. Although the shops relied on Tim's name and personality for their commercial success, Tim never really enjoyed the public appearances—he was usually a bit shy. As the business grew more successful, Ron kept asking Tim for more of his time. But between hockey, travel, and the company, Tim found he had far too much to do, and his family life was suffering.

Tim Hortons *was originally called* Tim Horton. *The four donuts represented Tim and Lori's four daughters.*

Tim Tales

Anyone with such a long career is always the subject of great stories. Players often played tricks on each other or held initiations for younger players. As his career developed and the pressures grew, Tim sometimes got carried away after drinking a few beers. He was known for knocking down hotel room doors in order to say "Good night" to fellow players. At first it was funny, but often there was serious damage. One player estimated that Tim's pranks may have resulted in 60 doors being knocked down.

Lori and Tim had marriage problems and she was particularly concerned about his drinking. As the girls grew older, the family faced the challenge of raising teens. Lori herself was prescribed an antidepressant medicine that was later found to be highly addictive. Today, that medication is banned. Lori spent nearly twenty years from 1965–84 fighting the ravages of this addiction. Sadly, just when so much seemed to be going well for the Hortons, the pressures of family, career, and business almost overwhelmed them all.

TIM HORTON
SABRES
defense

Tim did not stay in Pittsburgh for long. Once again, he was thinking about retirement, when he got a new offer. Punch Imlach had resurfaced as the coach and general manager of an expansion team—the Buffalo Sabres. Imlach valued Tim's commitment to

One personal change for Tim after the 1967 series was the loss of his famous "brushie". The Horton brush cut was almost a trademark, but in the long-haired '60s and '70s, his daughters felt it was horribly out of date. In fact, with his many scars and scrapes showing through the short hair, his family felt he looked a bit like Frankenstein.

team play and felt his young team would benefit from Tim's veteran experience. Tim won another good contract that included some time off to take care of his business. He earned $150,000 and a fast new car—a Ford Pantera. Although he was nearing the end of his career, things were going well for the great defenseman.

Last Stop for the Ice General

Imlach saw Tim as an "Ice General." He could steady younger players and help guide them to victory. Even when he was in his 40s, Tim quickly proved his worth to his junior teammates. Once again, his own teammates recognized his contribution when they voted him MVP. Although he kept promising to retire, he kept returning to the ice. Buffalo was to be his last team.

Chapter Eight

The Last Night

*In his last game, Tim resisted being pulled in the third period. The team
sagged without him, and he felt that he, personally, had lost the game.
In this picture, if you look carefully, you can see the swelling on his
right cheek that he received from his injury in practice earlier that day.*

On February 21, 1974, the storied life of the great Tim Horton came to a crashing end. It was 4:30 in the morning on the Queen Elizabeth Highway near St. Catharines, Ontario when his speeding Ford Pantera flew off the highway in a deadly somersault. Tim was not wearing a seatbelt—a tragic mistake, although seatbelt use was not mandatory at that time—and his body was thrown 123 feet through the air. Police found a weak pulse when they arrived at the scene of the accident, but the famous hockey player was declared dead on arrival at the local hospital. It was a sad end to a career of such success and hard work. He left a wife, four children, a thriving business, and friends and colleagues in the hockey capitals of North America.

Tim had had a mixed day. He had been hit in the face by a slapshot during practice with the Sabres. In pain and on painkillers, he played his last game in Toronto. The Leafs won the match against the Sabres, but not because Horton didn't give an all-out effort in spite of his injury. In fact, although he was mercifully pulled from the game early, he still managed to be named the third star. He was bothered that he had not been able to contribute more and seemed to blame himself a little for the loss.

> **"I watched that game Wednesday night and Tim was the best defenseman on the ice, by plenty. He didn't carry the puck on the ice as much, but in his own end he was still the boss."**
>
> Allan Stanley in *Remembering Tim Horton*

The 44-year-old's scarred body had seen better days. It was late, and he was tired and in pain. He had a final conversation with Punch Imlach about the game. Tim insisted on driving his beloved Ford Pantera from Toronto to Buffalo along the QEW rather than going back on the team bus.

Instead of going straight home, he dropped into the Oakville office of Tim Horton Donuts. He was still juggling his two careers even on the last day of his life. After staying a while and having a drink with Ron Joyce, perhaps to ease his pain, he got into his car and drove. He drove fast. He had always loved fast cars. On this late night, speed, alcohol, medication, and fatigue overwhelmed the giant. We can learn much from Tim's career, values, and hard work. Regrettably, we can also learn from his death.

Tim's teammates were devastated by the news of his death.

A few mistakes ended his life and career. We shall never know what other experiences and accomplishments might have lain before him. His life was full but still very short.

Impact

When the news came out, Tim's family and friends and the whole hockey world were shocked and devastated. His teammates on the Buffalo Sabres found it hard to play since their soul and leader had been taken so unexpectedly. Some players found it impossible to participate in the next scheduled game. These tough hockey players were simply overwhelmed by losing Tim. The Sabres team that was assembled for the next game wore black armbands and held a minute of silence in his honor. At his funeral, the pallbearers were his fellow teammates from the great Maples Leaf team of 1967.

Chapter Nine

A Full Life

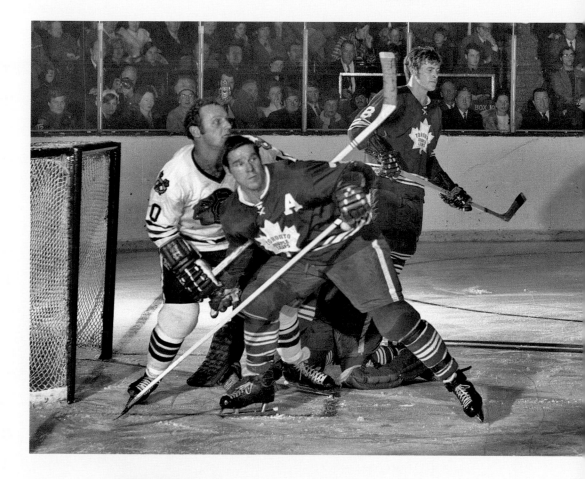

lthough Tim's life was cut tragically short, his record as a father, businessman, player, and friend stands for itself.

Business

Being a father, husband, and hockey star, while also establishing the roots of one of North America's most successful and beloved businesses, is remarkable. Tim had always worked hard, even while playing hockey. He physically helped to build some of the first stores in the Tim Hortons franchise. On his last night, he even found time to drop in at the office.

The Tim Hortons Empire

Although Tim's wife and Ron Joyce no longer own and run the company, it is still tremendously successful. Ron Joyce bought half of the company in 1964 for a mere $12,000. In 1974, after Tim's death, Ron bought the rest of the company from Lori Horton for a million dollars. In 1995, Tim Hortons merged with Wendy's International and began a rapid expansion into the United States. In 2001, Ron Joyce sold his shares in the combined company for US$250 million! By March of 2006, Tim Hortons (**www.timhortons.com**) was a separate company once again and placed for public sale.

The Tim Horton Children's Foundation

The Tim Horton Children's Foundation was established in 1974 by Ron Joyce, Tim's business partner in order "to honour Tim Horton's love for children and his desire to help those less fortunate." The Foundation provides a camp experience for kids from poorer homes and communities. In 2006, 11,000 kids were welcomed into the 6 camps run by the Foundation. Tim would likely be very pleased with this work done in his memory and bearing his name.

Investors all over North America and the world paid a total of $5.5 billion dollars to own a piece of the business that Tim Horton had started. From that first Tim Horton donut store that opened in Hamilton in 1964, the chain that Tim Horton and Ron Joyce began has expanded to a business empire that in 2009 numbered 3000 Canadian stores and a growing U.S. business of 500 stores. The company even opened a store in the famed Times Square in New York. Its headquarters is in Oakville, Ontario.

Timbits Minor Sports

Long after Tim's death, the company developed another program tied to Tim's first love—sports. As of 2009, Tim Hortons sponsors 200,000 kids between the ages of 4-8 who play on hockey, soccer, lacrosse, t-ball, baseball, and ringette teams across Canada and in the United States. The goal of the games is to foster fun and participation, rather than emphasize winning and losing. Participants are given t-shirts and jerseys, and sometimes they get the chance to play short scrimmages during the intermission at NHL games.

Sponsorships

The company also serves as a partner and sponsor of teams and events in the NHL and CFL. Cycling, fishing, and curling are a few of the other sports that are associated with Tim Hortons.

Kandahar

In 2006, a huge Hercules aircraft touched down at a Canadian military base in Kandahar, Afghanistan. At that time, about 2300 Canadian soldiers were serving in Afghanistan to help defeat the Taliban and build a new life for the people of Afghanistan. It has been a very dangerous mission that has cost many Canadian lives. Far from home, the soldiers especially missed their Tim Hortons donuts and coffee.

When the aircraft's doors opened, instead of standard food, supplies, or tanks, out rolled a Tim Hortons truck! The shop was opened to the troops on Canada Day 2006.

Timeline

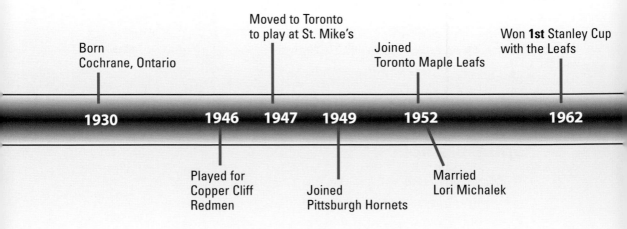

Born
Cochrane, Ontario — 1930

Played for
Copper Cliff
Redmen — 1946

Moved to Toronto
to play at St. Mike's — 1947

Joined
Pittsburgh Hornets — 1949

Joined
Toronto Maple Leafs — 1952

Married
Lori Michalek

Won **1st** Stanley Cup
with the Leafs — 1962

Hockey

In a brilliant career that spanned 22 seasons and 1,446 games, Tim Horton achieved what many players can only dream about. His record as a hockey player speaks for itself. He is viewed as one of the legends of the game.

However, as impressive as his long career is, it cannot by itself tell us of Tim's strength, ambition, work ethic, sense of humor, and dedication to his teammates, friends, and family.

When asked how he was still able to play at such an advanced age (for a hockey player), he simply noted, "All it takes is hard work."

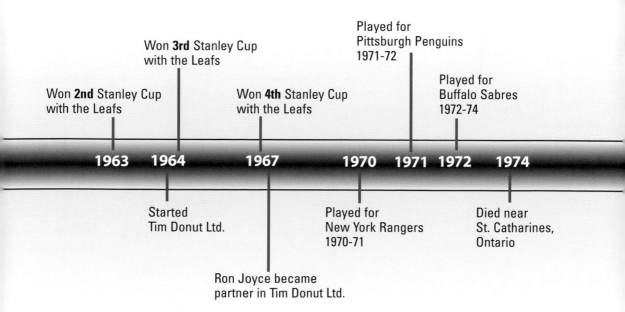

Won **2nd** Stanley Cup
with the Leafs

Won **3rd** Stanley Cup
with the Leafs

Won **4th** Stanley Cup
with the Leafs

Played for
Pittsburgh Penguins
1971-72

Played for
Buffalo Sabres
1972-74

1963   1964   1967   1970   1971 1972   1974

Started
Tim Donut Ltd.

Played for
New York Rangers
1970-71

Died near
St. Catharines,
Ontario

Ron Joyce became
partner in Tim Donut Ltd.

- First All-Star Team Defense (1964, 1968, 1969)

- Second All-Star Team Defense (1954, 1963, 1967)

- Four Stanley Cup Championship Teams (Toronto Maple Leafs)

- The Tim Horton Arena in Cochrane was renamed as a memorial to the great legend after renovations were made to include an auditorium. (1975)

- Inducted into Hockey Hall of Fame. (1977)

- The Buffalo Sabres retired Horton's Number 2 during the 1995-96 season.

- The Toronto Maple Leafs honored Tim's Number 7 during the 1995-96 season.

- In 1996, the people of Cochrane decided to honor him for the fame he brought to his hometown. They built a museum where more than 800 mementoes of the player are housed in the #137 Locomotive and associated coaches.

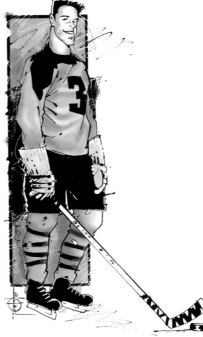

Tim's Official Stats

Season	Club	League	GP	G	A	TP	PIM	+/-	GP	G	A	TP	PIM
1946-47	Copper Cliff Jr. Redmen	NOJHA	9	0	0	0	14		5	0	1	1	0
1947-48	St. Michael's Majors	OHA-Jr.	32	6	7	13	137						
1948-49	St. Michael's Majors	OHA-Jr.	32	9	18	27	95						
1949-50	Toronto Maple Leafs	NHL	1	0	0	0	2		1	0	0	0	2
1949-50	Pittsburgh Hornets	AHL	60	5	18	23	83						
1950-51	Pittsburgh Hornets	AHL	68	8	26	34	129		13	0	9	9	16
1951-52	Toronto Maple Leafs	NHL	4	0	0	0	8						
1951-52	Pittsburgh Hornets	AHL	64	12	19	31	146		11	1	3	4	16
1952-53	Toronto Maple Leafs	NHL	70	2	14	16	85						
1953-54	Toronto Maple Leafs	NHL	70	7	24	31	94		5	1	1	2	4
1954-55	Toronto Maple Leafs	NHL	67	5	9	14	84						
1955-56	Toronto Maple Leafs	NHL	35	0	5	5	36		2	0	0	0	4
1956 57	Toronto Maple Leafs	NHL	66	6	19	25	72						
1957-58	Toronto Maple Leafs	NHL	53	6	20	26	39						
1958-59	Toronto Maple Leafs	NHL	70	5	21	26	76		12	0	3	3	16
1959-60	Toronto Maple Leafs	NHL	70	3	29	32	69		10	0	1	1	6
1960-61	Toronto Maple Leafs	NHL	57	6	15	21	75		5	0	0	0	0
1961-62	Toronto Maple Leafs	NHL	70	10	28	38	88		12	3	13	16	16
1962-63	Toronto Maple Leafs	NHL	70	6	19	25	69		10	1	3	4	10
1963-64	Toronto Maple Leafs	NHL	70	9	20	29	71		14	0	4	4	20
1964-65	Toronto Maple Leafs	NHL	70	12	16	28	95		6	0	2	2	13
1965-66	Toronto Maple Leafs	NHL	70	6	22	28	76		4	1	0	1	12
1966-67	Toronto Maple Leafs	NHL	70	8	17	25	70		12	3	5	8	25
1967-68	Toronto Maple Leafs	NHL	69	4	23	27	82	+20					
1968-69	Toronto Maple Leafs	NHL	74	11	29	40	107	+14	4	0	0	0	7
1969-70	Toronto Maple Leafs	NHL	59	3	19	22	91	+4					
1969-70	New York Rangers	NHL	15	1	5	6	16	-7	6	1	1	2	28
1970-71	New York Rangers	NHL	78	2	18	20	57	+28	13	1	4	5	14
1971-72	Pittsburgh Penguins	NHL	44	2	9	11	40	+5	4	0	1	1	2
1972-73	Buffalo Sabres	NHL	69	1	16	17	56	+12	6	0	1	1	4
1973-74	Buffalo Sabres	NHL	55	0	6	6	53	+5					
	NHL Totals		**1446**	**115**	**403**	**518**	**1611**		**126**	**11**	**39**	**50**	**183**

Index

Image Credits

Bibliography

CBC Digital Archives

> *Tim Hortons: Coffee, Crullers and Canadiana*
> archives.cbc.ca/lifestyle/food/topics/3525/

> *Tim Horton gets emotional in '67*
> archives.cbc.ca/sports/hockey/clips/15201/

> *Life and Times: Tim Horton*
> www.cbc.ca/lifeandtimes/horton.html

Hockey Hall of Fame
http://www.hhof.com/

Horton, Lori and Tim Griggs.
In Loving Memory: A Tribute to Tim Horton.
Toronto: ECW Press, 1997.

Hunter, Douglas.
Open Ice: The Tim Horton Story.
Toronto: Penguin Books, 1995.

MacInnis, Craig (editor).
Remembering Tim Horton.
Toronto: Stoddart Publishing Co. Ltd., 2000.

Also available from
Fitzhenry & Whiteside:

Robert Munsch

Frank B. Edwards